Practical Pre-School Books

KU-795-998

The Early Years Foundation Stage in practice

by Liz Wilcock

Contents

Published by Practical Pre-School Books, A Division of MA Education Ltd, St Jude's Church, Dulwich Road, Herne Hill, London, SE24 0PB.

Tel: 020 7738 5454

www.practicalpreschoolbooks.com

© MA Education Ltd 2012

Design: Alison Cutler **fonthill**creative 01722 717043

All images © MA Education Ltd. All photos taken by Lucie Carlier.

ISBN 978-1-907241-25-3

LEARNING
RESOURCES

189605

Introduction

Department for Education (DfE)

On 6 July 2010, Children's Minister Sarah Teather asked Dame Clare Tickell, Chief Executive of Action for Children, to carry out an independent review of the Early Years Foundation Stage (EYFS), to consider how this could be less bureaucratic and more focused on supporting children's early learning.

The review covered four main areas:

- scope of regulation – whether there should be one single framework for all early years providers

- learning and development – looking at the latest evidence about children's development and what is needed to give them the best start at school

- assessment – whether young children's development should be formally assessed, at a certain age, and what this should cover

- welfare – the minimum standards to keep children safe and support their healthy development.

The review reported on 30 March 2011, with a view to implementing any changes from September 2012 onwards.

So, what are the changes that we need to explore?

The Department for Education states that the reforms will:

- reduce paperwork and bureaucracy

- strengthen partnerships between parents and professionals

- focus on the three prime areas of learning most essential for children's readiness for future learning and healthy development

- simplify assessment at age five, and

- provide for early intervention where necessary, through the introduction of a progress check at age two.

There are changes to the welfare requirements too.

To emphasise the importance of safeguarding, the welfare requirements are now the **Safeguarding and Welfare Requirements**

In section 3 of the revised Statutory Guidance document, pages 13-29, there is detailed guidance on what <u>must</u> be done to ensure that all legal requirements can be met.

In short:

1. *Child protection:* the revised EYFS includes examples of adults' behaviour which might be signs of abuse and neglect. If they become aware of any such signs, staff should respond appropriately in order to safeguard children.

2. *The EYFS:* it now requires that safeguarding policies and procedures must cover the use of mobile phones and cameras in the setting.

3. *Suitable people:* the requirements for providers to check the suitability of managers have been simplified. From September 2012, providers will be responsible for obtaining criminal record disclosures on managers. Currently, Ofsted obtain these disclosures.

4. *Staff qualifications, training, support and skills:* a requirement has been introduced in relation to staff supervision. Providers must give staff opportunities for coaching and training, mutual support, teamwork, continuous improvement and confidential discussion of sensitive issues.

5. *The requirement for childminders:* to complete training in the EYFS. This has been strengthened; childminders will be required to complete the training before they register with Ofsted.

6. *Staff to child ratios:* there is a clarification of the circumstances in which there may be exceptions to the staff to child ratios for childminders caring for children of mixed ages.

Press notice: 30 March 2011, Department for Education

'Dame Clare Tickell is today recommending that the Early Years Foundation Stage (EYFS) is radically slimmed down to make it easier to understand, less burdensome and more focused on making sure children start school ready to learn.

Setting out her recommendations, Dame Clare says that while parents and early years professionals agree that the EYFS has had a positive impact on children's outcomes and helped to raise standards, in its current form there is far too much time spent filling in forms and not enough interacting with children. She says the EYFS needs to be simplified and made even more accessible for parents and practitioners.

Dame Clare Tickell said:

The earliest years in a child's life are absolutely critical. Next to a loving and stable home environment, high quality early years education is one of the most important factors in a child's development. It's clear that the current EYFS has helped to improve outcomes and is popular with parents and professionals who welcome a framework that lets them know how children are developing.

But it's far from perfect. The current EYFS is cumbersome, repetitive and unnecessarily bureaucratic. And it isn't doing enough to engage parents in their child's development or make sure children are starting school with the basic skills they need to be ready to learn.

My recommendations will help give those professionals more freedom and are designed to make the entire system work better for children, professionals and parents. I hope my review leads to a slimmer, more resilient EYFS, that makes sure every child has the best possible start in life'.

Introduction

7. *Safety and suitability of premises, environment and equipment:* the requirements in relation to risk assessment have been adjusted to clarify that it is for providers to judge whether a risk assessment needs to be recorded in writing.

The Statutory Framework document makes clear what the EYFS seeks to provide:

- **quality and consistency** in all early years settings, so that every child makes good progress and no child gets left behind

- **a secure foundation** through learning and development opportunities which are planned around the needs and interests of each individual child and are assessed and reviewed regularly

- **partnership working** between practitioners and with parents and/or carers

- **equality of opportunity** and anti-discriminatory practice, ensuring that every child is included and supported.

The **learning and development requirements** cover:

- the *areas of learning and development* which must shape activities and experiences (*educational programmes*) for children in all early years settings

- the *early learning goals* that providers must help children work towards (the knowledge, skills and understanding children should have at the end of the academic year in which they turn five), and

- *assessment arrangements* for measuring progress (and requirements for reporting to parents and/or carers).

So, what has happened to the four theme headings and their principles?

The key point is that there are no changes to the themes and their principles – these remain as the basis of the EYFS:

- every child is a **unique child**, who is constantly learning and can be resilient, capable, confident and self-assured

- children learn to be strong and independent through **positive relationships**

- children learn and develop well in **enabling environments**, in which their experiences respond to their individual needs and there is a strong partnership between practitioners and parents and/or carers, and

- **children develop and learn in different ways and at different rates**. The framework covers the education and care of all children in early years provision, including children with special educational needs and disabilities.

What has happened to the Every Child Matters agenda?

The Department for Education states that:

The Coalition Government remains absolutely committed to improving outcomes for children and families, and providing excellence in children's services. The Every Child Matters programme had a positive impact on many children's lives. However, the programme for the Coalition Government is underpinned by a desire for localism, transparency, increased trust in professionals, and reduced bureaucracy. While the fundamental framework of Every Child Matters is sound, it is not the role of Government to tell local authorities how to implement. However, if it is valuable locally or organisationally for practitioners to have a consistent and recognisable label to operate under, then we would expect them to continue using the Every Child Matters brand.

So, what does this actually mean?

The ECM agenda is not forgotten, in other words, Every Child *does* Matter!

You can continue to use the brand (as the Department for Education describes it) as you know it, as a recognisable label. We are all familiar with the Every Child Matters agenda – it is something we are all aware has broadly underpinned the four themes of the EYFS since the framework was introduced to us in 2008. The new administration have not made written reference to ECM within the revised EYFS document as they are placing greater emphasis on less bureaucracy, and less paperwork. Of course, as professionals we all need to follow developments as the Coalition Government looks to the future for the ECM agenda, but one thing is worth remembering – the government is committed to improving outcomes for all children within the EYFS.

The revised EYFS tells us that:

A Unique Child + Positive Relationships
+ Enabling Environments = Learning and Development.

This book will support practitioners in their understanding of the revised EYFS. It covers:

Section One
Exploring ways of putting the EYFS principles into practice

Section Two
Supporting children in their learning

Section Three
Leadership and support
Quality in the setting
Professional development

The revised EYFS Statutory Framework is supported by non-statutory guidance that has been produced by the Department for Education's voluntary partners.

This guidance includes:

The Development Matters document that:

'might be used by early years settings throughout the EYFS as a guide to making best-fit judgements about whether a child is showing typical development for their age, may be at risk of delay or is ahead for their age'.

The Know How document that:

'is intended to support practitioners within early years settings who are undertaking the EYFS progress check at age two. The progress check has been introduced to enable earlier identification of development needs so that additional support can be put into place'.

These documents and other supporting guidance can be found on:

- www.education.gov.uk/publications

- www.foundationyears.org.uk

The information for this book is sourced from:

- *The Early Years: Foundations for life, health and learning* (2011)

- *The EYFS revised framework, with references to the EYFS* (2008)

- Department for Education (www.education.gov.uk)

- Ofsted (www.ofsted.gov.uk)

- Progress Matters

- (EYQISP) Early Years Quality Improvement Support Programme.

Section One: Exploring ways of putting the EYFS principles into practice

A Unique Child

Every child is a unique child who is constantly learning and can be resilient, capable, confident and self-assured.

Let's look at how you can:

- understand and observe each child's development and learning, assess progress and plan for next steps

- support babies and children to develop a positive sense of their own identity and culture

- identify any need for additional support that will help each child to reach their potential

- keep children safe

- value and respect all children and families equally.

Young children are vulnerable. They develop resilience when their physical and psychological well-being is protected by adults. Babies and young children have little sense of danger – they can only learn how to assess the risks they may face with the guidance from adults. Young children need to know the limits and boundaries on what they may or may not do for their own safety and for the safety of others. Practitioners need to guard against making choices for the children. When you observe children, you can establish their interests and so you can effectively plan for their next steps in their learning. You may also notice when a child is struggling and may be in need of additional support.

Think about how you:

- actively listen to and observe children

- constantly assess risks and allow children to assess risk too

- share concerns

- keep the setting clean, safe and secure

- update training regularly

- maintain relevant documentation

- ensure premises, equipment and materials are appropriate for the children attending the setting

- foster children's curiosity, drives and adventurous spirits; help them to recognise boundaries; teach them how to make choices, and keep themselves safe.

Children's health is an integral part of their emotional, mental, social, environmental and spiritual well-being and is supported by attention to these aspects. Children really do thrive when their physical and emotional needs are met. Being physically healthy is not simply about having nutritious food. It also includes having a clean and safe environment, healthcare and mental stimulation.

Making friends and getting on with others helps children to feel positive about themselves and others. Remember that children should be treated equally. This does not mean to treat children in the same way – it is all about treating every child as an individual, and meeting their needs accordingly. No two children are the 'same'. We can support children's understanding of the differences between individuals and groups in society by giving children accurate information about, for example, gender, racial origins, culture, disability and physical appearances. We need to acknowledge that children do notice differences.

Ensure that you promote children's self esteem by valuing children for who they are – show respect for the child and their family and their backgrounds. Praising children for their efforts/achievements boosts confidence.

Positive Relationships

Children learn to be strong and independent through positive relationships. Warm, trusting relationships with knowledgeable adults supports children's learning more effectively than any amount of resources.

Let's look at how you can:

- be warm and loving, and foster a sense of belonging

- be sensitive and responsive to the child's needs, feelings and interests

- be supportive of the child's own efforts and independence

- be consistent in setting clear boundaries

- provide stimulation

- build on key person relationships in early years settings.

Every interaction is based on caring professional relationships and respectful acknowledgement of the feelings of children and their families. At times, we all experience strong emotions as we deal with difficult or stressful events. Children gradually learn to understand and manage their feelings with support from the adults around them. As children develop socially, they begin to choose best friends and show preferences for the children they wish to play with. Professional relationships are based on friendliness towards parents, but not necessarily friendships with parents. Respect for others is the basis of good relationships. Babies and children learn who they are and what they can accomplish through relationships. Think about the balance you need to strike between 'nurture and structure'. Both have an important part to play in your setting as you plan to meet the care and learning needs of the children. Nurture is about adults offering love and support so that children feel loved and accepted, receive warmth and affection and they are given time, so that they have their physical and emotional health protected and have their efforts praised. Structure is about adults setting boundaries so that children know the rules and what is expected of them, but also that adults are flexible within these boundaries. Children need space to express themselves and their opinions. They feel safe to try new things within the environment and make their own mistakes – they are learning to be independent.

Children need to understand about their feelings and how to manage them. Accept children's feelings and reassure them that they can express them. When you respond to their outbursts, ensure that children understand that their behaviour does not threaten your relationship with them. Share and talk about picture books and stories that explore feelings. Help children to understand and take account of the needs of other children in the setting, for example, by discussing with older children the needs of babies and toddlers in the group, or by teaching children how to sign so that they can communicate with a child who has a hearing impairment. Help all children to appreciate their own personal characteristics and preferences and those of other children. Identify children's chosen playmates and consider how effectively the ways that you group children enable them to build and sustain friendships. Give particular attention to children who appear withdrawn.

> Think about how you:
>
> - support children to learn about others, through their relationships. How do you help them to become aware that others may have different needs, feelings and ideas from their own?
>
> - guide children, through friendships, to develop their interpersonal skills
>
> - foster children's emotional and social development
>
> - help children feel safe and able to express their feelings
>
> - respond with respect to children and parents.

Enabling Environments

Children learn and develop well in enabling environments, in which their experiences respond to their individual needs and there is a strong partnership between practitioners, parents and carers.

Let's look at how you can:

- value the families that you come into contact with

- value each child's learning

- provide stimulating resources that are relevant to the children's cultures and communities

- offer rich learning opportunities through play and playful teaching

- support and challenge children to take risks and explore.

A rich and varied environment supports children's learning and development. It gives them the confidence

to explore and learn in secure and safe, yet challenging, indoor and outdoor spaces.

When children feel confident in the environment, they are willing to try things out, knowing that their efforts are valued. Outdoor environments offer children freedom to explore, use their senses, and be physically active. For some children, the indoor environment is like a second 'home', providing a place for activity, rest, eating and sleeping.

There is no ideal environment – babies and young children's interests change all the time, and so the environment should change in response to the children's current interests. Resources that stimulate interest in what is happening in the local community and also resources that reflect the cultures represented in your setting will also change as you consider ways to support the children's learning.

Many practitioners consider what they can provide for the children, indoors and outside, however, the emotional environment is equally important. When children feel secure and confident, they develop their

Think about how you:

● plan to support children in your environment. Do you consider both the indoor and outdoor environments? What thought do you give to the emotional environment?

● make sure that you have sufficient opportunities for children to make choices in the environment

● involve parents

● develop flexible routines to meet the needs of the children

● ensure that transitions are smooth.

own thinking and scope for their independent learning. When practitioners bring together their knowledge about individual children, and knowledge about how they learn best, they can plan to provide for the next steps.

Section Two: Supporting children in their learning

In the first section of this book, we looked at A Unique Child, Positive Relationships and Enabling Environments. In this section, we will explore the fourth theme of the EYFS – Learning and Development. Remember that the EYFS is not all about children's learning – it is about the care provided for the children too, and the suitability of the people responsible for the care.

There have been some significant changes in the revised EYFS that we need to consider.

1. Firstly, we should remember that:

A Unique Child + Positive Relationships
+ Enabling Environments = Learning and Development

What does this actually mean? When we effectively support each child in their learning, meet each child's needs, work closely with parents and carers, and provide a safe and stimulating environment, we are in a good position to help a child develop and progress. How can you provide support for children with additional needs in your setting? Think about each child and their individual needs.

A Unique Child

'Uniqueness' is about understanding and addressing the needs of all children.

Identifying disabled children in the setting

The Disability Discrimination Act (DDA), which is now incorporated into The Equalities Act 2010, defines a disabled person as someone who has a physical or mental impairment which has a substantial and long-term adverse effect on his or her ability to carry out normal day-to-day activities, affecting either:

- mobility

- manual dexterity

- physical co-ordination, continence

- ability to lift, carry or otherwise move everyday objects

- speech

- hearing or eyesight

- memory or ability to concentrate, learn or understand, and/or

- perception of risk of physical danger.

Positive Relationships

This is about integrated working with parents, health and social partners and linking with Early Support.

Early Support

Early Support is a government programme to improve quality, consistency and coordination of services for young disabled children and their families. It is targeted at families with children under five, with additional support needs associated with disability or emerging special educational needs. The programme promotes partnership working with families which can be applied across the age range.

Enabling Environments

This is about working together with partners to devise a planned approach to removing barriers, sharing and combining resources to give the child a positive start to development and education

Statutory Requirements

All schools have duties under the Equalities Act 2010 to:

- not treat disabled children 'less favourably', and

- make reasonable adjustments for disabled children.

The duties also place similar obligations on all services and early years settings that are not schools (such as nurseries, children centres and pre-school provision, including playgroups and childminders).

The SEN Code of Practice (CoP) helps early education settings, schools and LAs meet their responsibilities for children with special educational needs.

Learning and Development

This is about working with parents and LAs to ensure that plans are in place for continued access to learning and development on transition between settings.

Ensuring that your setting meets the requirement

- be aware and understand who your disabled children are

- assess the impact of your provision for access to learning and development for disabled children in your setting

- work with parents, health and social partners to support the child's development

- set out a priority plan such as Early Years Action Plan and Action Plan Plus which tailors support for the disabled child

- ensure plans are in place for transition either to another setting or to Key Stage 1, working with parents, setting/school and the local authority.

Engaging local authority support

- You may want to contact your local area SENCO or early years consultant to establish what training, support and resources are available.

Area of Learning	Aspects
Prime Areas	
Personal, Social, Emotional	Making relationships
	Self-confidence and self-awareness
	Managing feelings and behaviour
Communication and Language	Listening and attention
	Understanding
	Speaking
Physical Development	Moving and handling
	Health and self-care
Specific Areas	
Literacy	Reading
	Writing
Mathematics	Numbers
	Shape, space and measure
Understanding the World	People and communities
	The world
	Technology
Expressive Arts and Design	Exploring and using media and materials
	Being imaginative

2. Emphasis is now being placed on the way in which children learn, described within the revised EYFS as 'Characteristics of Effective Learning'. These are:

- Playing and exploring

- Active learning

- Creating and thinking critically

*'Your understanding of the different ways in which children learn is important – this knowledge will help you to continue to provide the best possible support. The EYFS describes **how** children learn through playing and exploring, through their active learning, through their creative instincts and by the way they think about things to make sense of what is happening or what they are experiencing. The three characteristics of learning are taken from the existing EYFS commitments and are typical of the way we all learn from babies to adulthood'.*

If you look on your EYFS poster, you will find the three Characteristics of Effective Learning in the fourth column – we know them as the commitments of the Learning and Development theme of the EYFS. Now, with greater emphasis on how children learn, these commitments have now been highlighted for us all to focus on the way in which children learn.

The Characteristics of Effective Learning – what do you need to consider?

Play and Exploration

What does this mean for children?

'Children's play reflects their wide ranging and varied interests. In their play children learn at their highest level. Play with peers is important for children's development'.

Children learn through their experiences:

- children may play alone or with others

- in their play, children use the experiences they have and extend them to build up ideas, concepts and skills

- while playing, children can express fears and re-live anxious experiences. They can try things out, solve problems and be creative and can take risks and use trial and error to find things out.

Children learn through adult involvement:

- play comes naturally and spontaneously to most children, though some need adult support. Support may be needed depending on the age of the child, or related to the child's abilities

- practitioners plan and resource a challenging environment where children's play can be supported and extended

- practitioners can extend and develop children's language and communication in their play through sensitive observation and appropriate intervention

- practitioners always intervene in play if it is racist, sexist or in any way offensive, unsafe, violent or bullying.

Children learn through the situations they find themselves in:

- children need plenty of space and time to play, both outdoors and indoors

Think about how you:

- provide flexible resources that can be used in many different ways to support children's play and exploration. These might include lengths of plastic guttering, tubing and watering cans near the sand and water play areas; lengths of fabric and clothes pegs in a box; large paintbrushes and buckets near the outside tap; boxes, clothes horses, old blankets and tablecloths to make dens and shelters

- observe children's play and help children to join in if they find it hard to be included, but watch and listen carefully before intervening

- find out how children play at home and value different cultural approaches to play

- value play which is based on people such as superheroes who may mean a lot to children, even if you do not appreciate them yourself!

- tell and read stories and encourage children to act them out.

- children who are allowed to play with resources and equipment before using them to solve a problem are more likely to solve the problem successfully

- making dens and dressing-up are an integral part of children's play and they don't require expensive resources

- role-play areas allow children to take on and rehearse new and familiar roles.

Active Learning

What does this mean for children?

'Children learn best through physical and mental challenges. Active learning involves other people, objects, ideas and events that engage and involve children for sustained periods'.

Let's consider the aspects of Active Learning.

Children's mental and physical involvement in their learning:

- to be mentally or physically engaged in learning, children need to feel at ease, secure and confident

- active learning occurs when children are keen to learn and are interested in finding things out for themselves

- when children are actively involved in learning they gain a sense of satisfaction from their explorations and investigations

- when children engage with people, materials, objects, ideas or events they test things out and solve problems. They need adults to challenge and extend their thinking.

Children's personalised learning:

- personalised learning involves planning for each child, rather than the whole group. It should also involve parents in their child's development and learning

- begin to plan for personalised learning by knowing about each child's well-being

- look at children's involvement in their learning as well as at the nature and quality of adult interactions in children's learning.

Think about how you:

- ensure children's well-being and involvement in learning by making each child feel secure and confident

- allow children some control over their learning

- can have realistic expectations of every child based on information from parents, what children themselves 'tell' you and from observation

- review your environment to ensure that it is interesting, attractive and accessible to every child so they can learn independently

- make learning plans for each child based on information gained from talking to them, their parents and your colleagues and by observing the child

- recognise that every child's learning journey is unique to them

- consider how you could make sufficient time to reflect on what has been observed about individual children and to reach conclusions about what has been learned

- consider how you could give children time to follow a particular line of enquiry given the constraints of your routines and access to areas such as outdoor spaces

- consider how you could gradually give children greater independence in their learning while retaining control over your learning programme.

Children's decision making:

- active learners need to have some independence and control over their learning to keep their interest and to develop their creativity

- as children become absorbed in finding out about the world through their explorations, investigations and questions they feel a sense of achievement, and their self esteem and confidence increase

- as children grow in confidence they learn to make decisions based on thinking things through in a logical way.

Creating and Thinking Critically

What does this mean for children?

'When children have opportunities to play with ideas in different situations and with a variety of resources, they discover connections and come to new and better understandings and ways of doing things. Adult support in this process enhances their ability to think critically and ask questions'.

How children can make connections in their learning:

- being creative involves the whole learning programme, not just the arts. It is not necessarily about making an end-product such as a picture, song or play

- children will more easily make connections between things they've learned if the environment encourages them to do so. For example, they need to be able to fetch materials easily and to be able to move them from one place to another

- effective practitioners value each child's culture and help them to make connections between experiences at home, the setting and the wider community

- it is difficult for children to make creative connections in learning when colouring in a worksheet or making a Diwali card just like everyone else's.

Developing children's understanding about their learning:

- this may be a long process – when children start to make new connections, for example, they may need to run, jump and walk through puddles many times to check out what happens. In this way they may begin to understand more about the effect of force on water (Knowledge of the World). They learn how to stay steady on their feet on a slippery surface (Physical Development). They might create a little dance about splashing (Creative Development) or say a rhyme such as 'Doctor Foster' (Communication and Language)

Think about how you:

- value what parents tell you about the way in which children behave and learn at home

- allow children to move equipment around your setting, indoors and outside, to extend their own play and learning

- ensure that there is a balance of adult-led and child-initiated activities

- document children's learning through photos and words. Use these to talk to children and parents about the learning that has taken place

- model being creative, for example, "I wasn't quite sure how to join this wheel on the car but then I thought about what we did last week. Can you remember what Kanisha did with her bus?"

- consider ways in which you could provide freedom for children to access resources while ensuring that they develop their understanding of the importance of tidying up and putting things back where they belong

- consider ways in which you could give very young children opportunities to express their ideas in all sorts of different ways – valuing movement and dance as highly as drawing and writing.

- effective practitioners record the processes that children go through. This will help everyone to see how the children's thinking is developing. Both children and adults can then talk about the learning that has taken place.

Sustained shared thinking:

This is about children being encouraged to make choices and to make decisions for themselves. Children need time and opportunities to think about things and develop their own ideas, supported by adults, who let children take the lead in their learning.

- in the most effective settings practitioners support and challenge children's thinking by getting involved in the thinking process with them

- sustained shared thinking involves the adult being aware of the children's interests and understandings and the adult and children working together to develop an idea or skill

- sustained shared thinking can only happen when there are responsive trusting relationships between adults and children

- the adult shows genuine interest, offers encouragement, clarifies ideas and asks open questions. This supports and extends the children's thinking and helps children to make connections in learning.

3. The Characteristics of Effective Learning underpin the prime and specific areas of learning. Previously, 6 areas of learning were our focus, and the message was clear that all 6 were interrelated and of equal importance. The revised EYFS has 7 areas of learning, separated into 'prime' and 'specific' areas. You will see that 'literacy' has been separated from 'communication and language' and become the seventh area of learning.

The prime areas are at the heart of each child's learning

From birth, babies begin to develop quickly in response to relationships and experiences. The prime areas continue to be at the core of learning throughout the EYFS – they run through and support learning in all other areas.

- **Personal, Social and Emotional Development.**
  This is all about developing children's self confidence and self esteem, that is – how children feel about themselves. It is also about helping children to manage their feelings and their behaviour, and supporting children to make relationships with others and to understand others too

- **Communication and Language.** This is all about developing children's listening and attention skills, helping children's understanding of language and developing their speaking skills

- **Physical Development.** This is all about helping children to be able to move around and be able to handle things. It is also about helping children to understand about health and their own self care.

The specific areas of development grow out of the prime areas, and provide important contexts for learning. Specific areas include essential skills and knowledge for children to participate successfully in society.

- **Literacy.** This is all about encouraging children to link sounds and letters and to begin to read and write

- **Mathematics.** This is all about providing children with opportunities to develop and improve their skills in counting, understanding and using numbers, calculating simple addition and subtraction problems; and to describe shapes, spaces, and measures. It is ultimately about supporting children to solve problems, helping them to develop their mathematical language, and to recognise, create and describe patterns. Mathematical learning can be supported, for example, by offering children the opportunity to explore shape, size and pattern during block play. Mathematical understanding can also be explored during daily routine, such as when preparing the table for lunch

- **Understanding the World.** This is all about guiding children to make sense of their physical world and their community

- **Expressive Arts and Design.** This is all about enabling children to explore and play with a wide range of media and materials, as well as providing opportunities and encouragement for sharing their thoughts, ideas and feelings through a variety of activities.

The prime and specific areas of learning support each other – it is not a case of the prime areas first and then the specific areas to follow. All 7 areas of learning are interrelated. On page 5 of the Development Matters document, you will see how the Characteristics of Effective Learning sit alongside the aspects associated with each area of learning. There has been a strong focus placed on the presentation of the revised EYFS – it has been written in clear, plain English.

4. Areas of learning – Aspects – Early Learning Goals – The Characteristics of Effective Learning.

Let's use an example from the Development Matters document to understand how it all comes together – refer to pages 8 and 9 of the document.

Title: Personal, Social and Emotional (showing the area of learning and the associated aspect).

Aspect: Making Relationships.

Three theme headings – A Unique Child (observing what a child is learning), Positive Relationships (what adults could do) and Enabling Environments (what adults could provide).

Find the ages of the children you are currently working with. Look at the first column – this is your guide under A Unique Child as to what you could see/observe the children learning. Look at the second column – this is your guide under Positive Relationships as to what you could do for the children. Look at the third column – this is your guide to what you could provide to support children's learning. Consider how the children are learning as you observe them and include this in your observation. Refer to the Characteristics of Effective Learning to assist you. At the end of page 9, you will find (in bold print) the Early Learning Goal for this aspect.

> ### Early Learning Goal
>
> *Children play co-operatively, taking turns with others. They take account of one another's ideas about how to organise their activity. They show sensitivity to others' needs and feelings, and form positive relationships with adults and other children.*

So, let's look at some ways in which you can support children in their play – with a focus on child-initiated play.

The term 'child-initiated play' is used frequently in the EYFS, because this way of learning is essential for children to help them understand the world around them. Children need to experience a wide range of learning opportunities – they learn from watching others and imitating them, as well as by their own exploring and experimenting. When children make decisions about their learning, that is, by deciding what they want to do, where they want to do it and what they will need in terms of resources, they are in control. Give them time to experiment with their ideas, offering support when necessary to help them to move their ideas on. Encourage the children to talk about their ideas and plans, suggest ways in which they may improve their skills and praise them for their efforts.

Your role in child-initiated play is important – you should strike a balance between intervening/offering support

and letting the children persevere with their chosen activity. Children are more likely to persist when they have worked things out for themselves, and then they will experience a sense of achievement.

'Where possible, link the indoor and outdoor environments so that children can move freely between them.' (EYFS, 2008)

The environment is important for children's learning – indoors and outside. Consider how you plan the space to enable easy access to resources.

Use clear labels to show where resources can be found (and returned to!). For rich learning experiences, children need to know that they can access resources from all areas.

Think about how you plan the environment, and how you will make resources available to the children.

Think about how you can plan the session to allow children the time they need to become engaged in play, either alone or with others.

Think about how you can allow children time to try things out and to repeat their play ideas, and learn from their mistakes.

What are the benefits of children planning their own learning experiences?

When children plan their own experiences, they become more interested in their learning. They are learning to communicate with others to solve problems and to take turns in conversation.

They will be learning how to take care of equipment, selecting equipment they need and using it independently. They will be learning to work as part of a group, or achieving a task by themselves.

Let's use water play as an example of children's learning – this is offered as part of your continuous provision (always available) but, as the Pre-School Learning Alliance explains, there are a lot of ways that children can learn from playing with water, beyond just for enjoyment!

Consider this extract taken from Pre-School Learning Alliance materials, *Sand and Water Play Activities*.

By careful observation the adult can provide experiences in sand and water play to challenge and extend young children's learning. From just splashing in water, they go on to:

- scooping it up

- pouring it out

- then to scooping it up and pouring it with increasing accuracy into another container

- filling the container without letting it overflow.

The observant adult needs to be aware of each individual child's progress so as to recognise when the child needs to be left alone to perfect a skill by repetition and when he or she needs help in moving on to the next stage.

"We must remember to build on the children's own play, not to direct operations from the outside."

Think about organising your water play equipment to maximise the learning opportunities for the children. Examples:

- the pond

- rainy/snowy/frosty days

- the seaside

- boats

- containers same shape

- containers same size

- absorption

- graded containers (1/2 litre, litre, 2 litre)

- wash day/washing up

- going through – sieves, funnels, tubing, spouts

- filling and pouring

- floating and sinking

Allow children to add other items to see what changes they can make. Examples:

- accessories made from the same material, e.g. wood, plastic, metal

- accessories which are the same colour, transparent, shiny

- accessories which are the same but different sizes, e.g. buckets, yogurt pots, funnels, plastic bottles, milk containers, plant pots, watering cans, boats

- specific numbers of items, e.g. 2 of everything

- colour with food colouring – allow the children to explore the effects that colour has when added to water – let the children mix colours of their choice

- scent with essential oil of lemon, lavender or peppermint (with caution and under supervison)

- add bubbles, colour the bubbles

- add glitter

- change the temperature – add ice cubes, freeze whole trays of water then pour on warm water

- thicken a tray of water with cornflour.

REMEMBER, water is potentially a danger to children.

Only a small quantity of water is needed for a child to drown, 2-3cms can cover a small nose. Always supervise water play, indoors and outside.

Let's consider how children can learn from play with water.

Personal, Social and Emotional Development

Children can:

- work independently

- co-operate, take turns and share equipment

- respect ideas of others

- experience the therapeutic value of water play

- learn how to use water safely – understand rules for water play

- talk about where water comes from

- enjoy the sensory nature of water by adding colours or other items, e.g. glitter

- learn how to work as part of a group, e.g. holding a funnel whilst another child pours

- extend imagination through the addition of other resources, e.g. boats, wood, sea shore items

- become confident at carrying out a range of activities in the water, e.g. pouring, blowing bubbles

- explore personal hygiene, e.g. using soap, washing dolls, clothes.

Language Development

Children can:

- describe the properties of water, e.g. wet, cold

- describe their actions and the actions of others, e.g. pouring, emptying, splashing

- extend vocabulary associated with water play

- describe similarities, differences and changes, e.g. which objects float/sink?

- explain what is happening when the water wheel is turning

- engage in role play as a fireman, plumber, adult washing clothes, dolls

- have access to books and rhymes connected to water, e.g. *Going to the Seaside*, *Mr Plug the Plumber*, *Rain*

- talk about their experiences in relation to display/ books about water play.

Physical Development

Children can:

- develop fine motor skills – manipulating tools, filling – pouring, emptying, stirring, squeezing, pushing, pulling

- develop hand/eye co-ordination, e.g. filling and emptying containers of different sizes, using a range of equipment with increasing skill and becoming aware of the flow speed of water and how they may control it

- be aware of the space in the water tray and be able to share it with others

- use tools, water and objects with increasing safety, e.g. be aware of what happens when a lot of water gets on the floor!

Early Mathematical Experiences

Children can:

- compare the amount of water in different containers by pouring from one to another

- understand and use mathematical language, e.g. full/empty, need more/less, heavy/light

- compare the size of containers, e.g. which is the biggest? which holds the most?

- talk about the shape of containers, e.g. straight sides, curved sides, circle at bottom

- understand and use positional words, e.g. pouring through, floating, on top of.

Early Experiences in Science and Technology

Children can:

- explore the properties of water, e.g. pour, run, drips

- ask questions about how things work and why they happen, e.g. stones in water, water wheels, flow of water, floating, sinking

- use their senses to investigate water, e.g. colour – sight; baby bath – smell; hot/cold – touch; bottled water – taste

- recognise the importance of water in personal hygiene

- observe how objects behave in water

- make predictions

- use cutting, folding, joining and building skills to make boats for water play

- explore ice in water.

Knowledge and Appreciation of the Environment

Children can:

- talk about water in local environment, home, rivers, pond, beach

- add equipment from local environment to stimulate imaginative play, e.g. shells, sea weed, pebbles, rocks, fishing nets, hoses, watering cans

- talk about occupations where water plays a significant role, e.g. fishermen, firemen, sailors, farmers, plumbers

- talk about animals and creatures that live in water, e.g. fish, crocodiles, sea-lions. Find books together encouraging interest about the world 'under water'

- understand the importance of hygiene using the water tray.

Creative/Aesthetic Development

Children can:

● observe colour change through adding paint or food dye

● introduce marbling techniques

● explore the effects on water by adding natural and man-made materials

● create underwater world to encourage imaginative play and language

● create sounds in the water, e.g. blowing, splashing, waving

● make musical instruments – filling bottles with water to different levels.

(By kind permission of Pre-School Learning Alliance *Small Messy Play Hands*, 2012)

5. Although there are seven areas of learning (as literacy has become a specific area of learning) there has been reduction in the number of aspects – previously there were 28 aspects associated with the areas of learning. There are now only 17, which are shown on the table on page 12 of this book. This has resulted in only 17 Early Learning Goals – significantly less than the 69 ELG's we considered previously. The Goals are highlighted at the end of each area of learning/aspect in your Development Matters document.

So, what does this mean for you? The key message is that there is <u>less</u> bureaucracy and <u>less</u> paperwork with the revised EYFS – your biggest challenge will be to focus on meaningful observations, rather than constantly recording everything you see the children doing. Practitioners have stated that there are expectations that they <u>must</u> do a certain number of observations each week.

Where have these expectations come from? It is this point that has raised much discussion – many practitioners have stated that they are constantly writing – taking them away from the direct care of the children. This was never the intention of the EYFS, however, perceived pressure from some local authority advisers and some Ofsted inspectors has almost created a monster in terms of paperwork. This had to be addressed, in the interests of practitioners and of course – the children!

The message is clear – the Statutory Framework states that:

● assessment plays an important part in helping parents, carers and practitioners to recognise children's progress, understand their needs, and to plan activities and support

● assessment should not entail prolonged breaks from interaction with children, nor require excessive paperwork. Paperwork should be limited to that which is absolutely necessary to promote children's successful learning and development.

So, how can this be achieved? Let's consider the importance of observations, and what you need to focus on.

6. Observation has always been an important part of the work we do. In short – we need to know how children are learning and how they are developing in order to help them progress. Of course, when we observe children, we can gauge their moods and feelings too as well as identifying their current interests. It is to what level we do this that really matters. Let's focus on what we need to know from the observations you write. Observations help us to focus on individuals, to note what motivates children and in what situation they develop best. We observe children so that we can share information with parents and colleagues in the best interests of the child. Observations also help us to identify when a child has reached (or not reached) a milestone, capturing the facts on a given date. You are then able to build up a picture of the child over time.

Parents want to know that their children are progressing, but they want your priority to be the love and care you provide for their children – the time you give them and the quality of the interactions.

When you observe the children, you should be able to do this with enjoyment, not because of expectation.

Practitioners need to know what the observation they have made says about the child in terms of their development. There is no point in writing for the sake of writing! Use a variety of observation methods, such as free narrative, checklists, target child and the tracker method.

If your setting uses one method only, explore other methods too.

Focus on what you need to know – significant moments in a child's development. Link these to the aspects of learning. When you review where a child is in terms of their development, you can see how you can continue to support the child, in other words, their next steps.

Remember, <u>HOW</u> children learn is important.

7. The role of the practitioner is to build on children's natural interest in exploration and to understand new things they encounter.

Let's look at how two different settings support children in their learning.

What do you provide to children in you setting that encourages them to explore and discover new things?

(Play and exploration)

Little Rainbows Day Nursery support their youngest children by giving them time to play and have fun! They work hard to build close relationships with the babies and younger children, giving them confidence to explore the environment, indoors and outside.

Victoria Park Nursery School offers an environment that is set up in an open, child-friendly way with resources at the children's level in 'learning bays'. Children are encouraged to be independent and explore at their own pace. A variety of resources are provided to allow children to re-visit over time. Children have long periods of uninterrupted time (free flow child-initiated time lasts for about 1 and ½ hrs) to allow children time to explore and develop their ideas in depth, indoors and outside.

How do you encourage children to learn together and from each other?

(Active learning)

Little Rainbows Day Nursery support their youngest children by allowing them to see how their carers work together as a team. The practitioners are involved with the babies' and younger children's play; they ask the children 'shall we all do this together?' They work at the children's physical level – usually on the floor!

Staff at Victoria Park Nursery School describe the ways in which older and more able children are encouraged to support younger less able peers; the best way to extend a child's learning is to allow them to show someone else how to do something, e.g. using the sticky tape! Children are in mixed age groups and all interact together, during child initiated free flow sessions. Children are praised, given positive reinforcement when they are working well together so

children aspire to this. Children are given the time to develop their relationships.

In terms of conflict resolution, a member of staff describes how two children wanted to play with the same train. The adult held the train and asked the children involved about the problem. The member of staff then encouraged the children to find a solution. This solution was repeated back to the two children by the adult to make sure that they both understood and agreed the solution. Remember – children will often come up with solutions that would not occur to adults, and they agree on the solution together.

How do you encourage children to solve problems and describe the problems they encounter?

(Creating and thinking critically)

Little Rainbows Day Nursery support their youngest children by providing activities that are realistic to each child's developmental steps, i.e. achievable challenges that do not cause frustration. They ask the children questions such as 'what happened?' to help them look at the situation.

Staff at Victoria Park Nursery School describe ways in which children are encouraged to solve their own problems, for example if the trolley gets stuck in the garden. Staff model problem solving as part of group time activities. Children are encouraged to take calculated risks and to accept that sometimes things do not work first time. Staff talk through different possibilities and encourage children to use prior knowledge. Children are encouraged to re-visit activities and learn from their mistakes.

On pages 6 and 7 of your Development Matters document you will see that the Characteristics of Effective Learning are shown in the column on the left, and guidance on how you can support A Unique Child, develop Positive Relationships, and provide an Enabling Environment is shown. These pages are useful in helping you understand the Characteristics of Effective Learning and how they fit in under the three theme headings.

8. There is a new requirement in the revised EYFS in relation to children aged two years.

   'When a child is aged between two and three, practitioners must review their progress, and provide parents and/or carers with a SHORT written summary of their child's development in the prime areas. This progress check must identify the child's strengths, and any areas where the child's progress is less than expected.

   Beyond the prime areas, it is for practitioners to decide what the written summary should include, reflecting the development level and needs of the individual child. The summary must highlight: areas in which a child is progressing well; areas in which some additional support might be needed; and focus particularly on any areas where there is a concern that a child may have a developmental delay.'

So, what do you need to do? Firstly, you need to be clear about WHY this requirement has come about. In the Know How document, there is useful information and guidance for you, written in plain English. There are a few points to consider:

a) If you have a developmental concern about a child, you should be in discussion with the parents about the concern, rather than waiting to highlight the concern in a progress check. If a parent has been fully consulted, there should be no unexpected (and potentially upsetting) records made.

b) Although the record is for parents, they do need to be made available for inspectors too. So, if a child starts in a setting at 2 years 9 months, having been in no other setting, would Ofsted expect a progress check to be done? There are a number of settings who take children as rising three's and they are unsure whether they could do this with relatively little knowledge of the child and family. The answer is clear – as this is a requirement of the revised EYFS, Ofsted will expect that settings will complete progress checks for all children between the ages of 2-3 years, even if they have only known the child for a few months. Of course, the progress check can only reflect what is known about the child, and clear reference should be made as to how long the child has been attending the setting.

c) There is emphasis on practitioners producing a SHORT written summary for each child. There are some examples in the Know How guide for you to consider using, although there is no set format. You can adapt these or devise your own forms. Ofsted inspectors will expect to see a copy of these summaries as evidence that you are meeting the requirement, however, Ofsted inspectors will not expect to see these in place within the first few months. Initially, the inspectors will be looking at whether providers are planning for when would be the best time for this assessment for individual children, and how they intend to report on this to parents. Plan ahead for how you may produce a summary report for your 2 year olds, so that, from September 2012, you will be able to describe to inspectors what you intend to do. Agree on the format you intend to use for your progress check and then start using it. Review it for effectiveness after a period of time and adapt if necessary.

9. At the end of the EYFS, the Profile will need to be completed for each child.

Child's name:	Date of birth:		Age in months	
Area of learning	**Early Learning Goal**	**Emerging**	**Expected**	**Exceeding**
Communication and Language	Listening and attention			
	Understanding			
	Speaking			
Physical Development	Moving and handling			
	Health and self-care			
Personal, Social and Emotional Development	Self-confidence and self-awareness			
	Managing feelings and behaviour			
	Making relationships			
Literacy	Reading			
	Writing			
Mathematics	Numbers			
	Shape, space and measures			
Understanding the World	People and communities			
	The world			
	Technology			
Expressive Arts, Designing and Making	Exploring and using media and materials			
	Being imaginative			

Learning characteristics	How (name of child) learns
Playing and exploring ● investigating and exploring ● representing experiences ● having a go	
Active learning ● being involved and absorbed ● keeping on trying ● enjoying achievement	
Creating and thinking critically ● having own ideas ● making links ● developing strategies	

In the final term of the year in which the child reaches age five, and no later than 30 June in that term, the EYFS Profile must be completed for each child. The Profile provides parents and carers, practitioners and teachers with a well-rounded picture of a child's knowledge, understanding and abilities, their progress against expected levels, and their readiness for Year 1. The Profile must reflect: ongoing observation; all relevant records held by the setting; discussions with parents and carers, and any other adults whom the teacher, parent or carer judges can offer a useful contribution.

Each child's level of development must be assessed against the early learning goals. Practitioners must indicate whether children are meeting expected levels of development, or if they are exceeding expected levels, or not yet reaching expected levels (emerging). This is the EYFS Profile.

At this time, the Profile is being trialled across 19 local authorities. Feedback from the trial will inform the development of the guidance materials which will be published in the Autumn term of 2012. The main change to the Profile is that the 117 scale points from the current profile will no longer apply – it is simply the focus on the 17 Early Learning Goals. Look at the table opposite on page 26 as a guide to what will need to be recorded. You will see that the Characteristics of Effective Learning are included, for a record to be made of the child's learning.

So, how do you know that the children are progressing in terms of their learning? Let's focus on how you can gather information about each child and how you can use that information to support each child's learning.

Firstly, we need to consider each child as 'unique':

● what do parents and carers tell you about the child?

● what play choices does the child make? When and how?

● what is the child really interested in? What does the child dislike?

● how are the views of the child sought?

● how does the child interact with other children and with adults? When, and with whom?

● how does the child respond to different situations and routines?

● how does the child tell you about his or her needs? How do you know when the child is happy?

● what can the child do at this stage? What is the child trying to do next? How does the child like to learn?

● what can professional partners contribute to your overall 'picture' of the child?

You can get the knowledge you need about the child from a mixture of observations and by your daily interactions/communications with the child and their parents, as well as other settings that the child may attend across the week. Your observations on the children in your setting will help you to think about how each of the children use different areas of the indoor and outdoor environment, what activities they are choosing, patterns of group or solitary play, and how different children or groups of children respond to the routines you have in place.

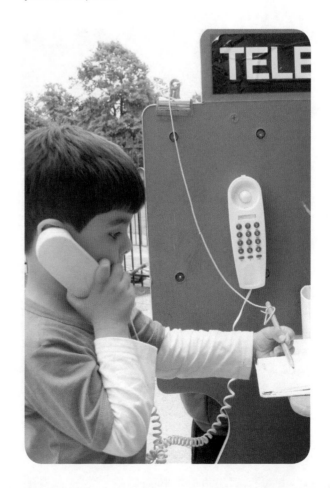

Never underestimate the importance of communication with parents, carers and other professionals – each have a role to play in ensuring that you have a good knowledge of the child. All contributions help to give you that 'picture' of the child.

Once you have gathered all the information you need, what do you do with it?

- use the knowledge you have to plan to meet the child's needs. This may mean, for example, adjusting the way in which you interact with the child, or introducing new experiences, changing routines, or rearranging the environment

- plan to support learning by following up on identified interests

- share your information with parents so that they can work together with you to best support their child

- liaise with other settings that child may be attending, so both you and the other setting better meet the

child's care and learning needs. Consider the benefits for the child in terms of his/her development when you liaise with others to share information.

Recording Progress

The table on page 29 is taken from Progress Matters; some of the content has been updated to relate to the Prime Areas of development for a baby.

You will see from the table that there is reference to the Birth to Three Matters Framework. This Framework contains useful guidance for those working with under 3's. You can access the Framework from the Foundation Years website (www.foundationyears.org.uk).

The Birth to Three Matters Framework, originally published in 2003, focuses on the care and learning of under 3's in all settings.

It comprises of 4 aspects and 4 components associated with each aspect. The Framework was warmly received and many practitioners will appreciate the guidance it provides within the revised EYFS.

What does the Framework contain?

ASPECT – A Strong Child

Component – **Me, Myself and I**

Realisation of own individuality

Including:

- Growing awareness of self

- Realising s/he is separate and different from others

- Recognising personal characteristics and preferences

- Finding out what s/he can do

Component – **Being Acknowledged and Affirmed**

Overview of development for Roza Robbins (DOB 09.06.08)

Evaluations drawn from discussions with parents, observational assessments and other professionals – include development points specific for this child

Contextual information – including languages, nationality, other care provided:	Some significant steps in development in the Prime Areas	First summary: 12.08.08	Second summary: 03.10.08	Third summary: 10.01.09
Started in setting 01.08.08 two days a week Both parents share care for Roza and take turns to bring her to nursery. She is their first child. Mother is Polish. Roza is allergic to cow's milk (21.09.08) and now has a formula prescribed by her GP Mother has taught staff some Polish songs and rhymes and recorded them on our MP3 player for us – Roza loves them and they also help when she is unsettled.	0-11 months – **PSE** Aspects – making relationships, self confidence and self awareness, and managing behaviour and feelings **CL** Aspects – listening and attention, understanding and speaking **PD** Aspects – moving and handling, health and self care **Birth to Three Matters** 0-8 months (heads up, lookers and listeners) Aspects – A strong child, skilful communicator, a competent learner, a healthy child	Roza has settled well at nursery. She kicks her legs when she is happy and clenches her fists when she is upset – needs a lot of reassurance at nappy changing time. Her mother has told us she is starting to smile at home and that she loves to lie outside under the tree. We have taken her to the park and she seems fascinated by the changes in shadow and light and moves her head and reaches out.	Roza has not been well. She has an allergy to cow's milk, has lost weight and is not the happy little girl of a couple of months ago. She cries easily and needs to be carried closely by her key worker for much of the day. She still smiles when her mum and dad come and has started to respond to some of our music tapes – going quiet and turning her head. At home she enjoys her mother singing Polish nursery rhymes – we are learning some at nursery.	Roza has made really good progress in CL and PSED this last month – everyone in nursery has noticed the difference in her ability to communicate what she wants and her confidence at trying new experiences. With support, she now enjoys lying on the mat and reaching out for the toys. She has a strong bond with her key worker, but also lifts up her arms for a cuddle with our midwife.

Experiencing and seeking closeness

Including:

- Needing recognition, acceptance and comfort

- Being able to contribute to secure relationships

- Understanding that s/he can be valued and important to someone

- Exploring emotional boundaries

Component – **Developing Self-assurance**

Becoming able to trust and rely on own abilities

Including:

- Gaining self assurance through a close relationship

- Becoming confident in what s/he can do

- Valuing and appreciating his/her own abilities

- Feeling self-assured and supported.

Component – **A Sense of Belonging**

Acquiring social confidence and competence

Including:

- Being able to snuggle in

- Enjoying being with familiar and trusted others

- Valuing individuality and contributions of self and others

- Having a role and identity within a group

ASPECT – A Skilful Communicator

Component – **Being Together**

Being a sociable and effective communicator

Including:

- Gaining attention and making contact

- Positive relationships

- Being with others

- Encouraging conversation

Component – **Finding a Voice**

Being a confident and competent language user

Including:

- The impulse to communicate

- Exploring, experimenting, labelling and expressing

- Describing, questioning, representing and predicting

- Sharing thoughts, feelings and ideas

Component – **Listening and Responding**

Listening and responding appropriately to the language of others

Including:

- Listening and paying attention to what others say

- Making playful and serious responses

- Enjoying and sharing stories, songs, rhymes and games

- Learning about words and meanings

Component – **Making Meaning**

Understanding and being understood

Including:

- Communicating meaning

- Influencing others

- Negotiating and making choices

- Understanding each other

ASPECT – A Competent Learner

Component – **Making Connections**

Connecting ideas and understanding the world

Including:

- Making connections through the senses and movement

- Finding out about the environment and other people

- Becoming playfully engaged and involved

- Making patterns, comparing, categorising, classifying

Component – **Being Imaginative**

Responding to the world imaginatively

Including:

- Imitating, mirroring, moving, imagining

- Exploring and re-enacting

- Playing imaginatively with materials using all the senses

- Pretend play with gestures and actions, feelings and relationships, ideas and words

Component – **Being Creative**

Responding to the world creatively

Including:

- Exploring and discovering

- Experimenting with sound, other media and movement

- Developing competence and creativity

- Being resourceful

Component – **Representing**

Responding to the world with marks and symbols

Including:

- Exploring, experimenting and playing

- Discovering that one thing can stand for another

- Creating and experimenting with one's own symbols and marks

- Recognising that others may use marks differently?

Aspect – A Healthy Child

Component – **Emotional Well-being**

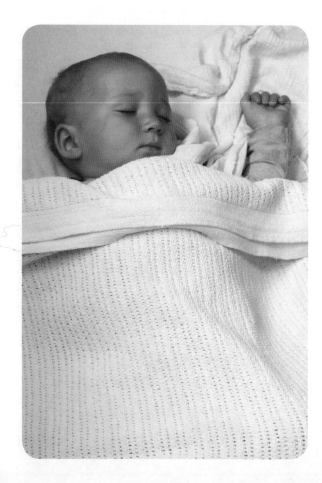

Emotional stability and resilience

Including:

- Being special to someone

- Being able to express feelings

- Developing healthy dependence

- Developing healthy independence

Component – **Growing and Developing**

Physical well-being

Including:

- Being well nourished

- Being active, rested and protected

- Gaining control of the body

- Acquiring physical skills

Component – **Keeping Safe**

Being safe and protected

Including:

- Discovering boundaries and limits

- Learning about rules

- Knowing when and how to ask for help

- Learning when to say no and anticipating when others will do so

Component – **Healthy Choices**

Being able to make choices

Including:

- Discovering and learning about his/her body

- Demonstrating individual preferences

- Making decisions

- Becoming aware of others and their needs

The Birth to Three Framework has age bands and descriptors of development for each age.

Heads Up, Lookers and Communicators (0-8 months)

During the first eight months, young babies react to people and situations with their whole bodies. They are also competent in observing and responding to their immediate environment and communicating with those around them.

Sitters, Standers and Explorers (8-18 months)

During the period from eight to eighteen months babies' exploration of the environment becomes more intentional. Increasing mobility and language development enable them to find out and understand more about their world.

Movers, Shakers and Players (18-24 months)

From eighteen to twenty four months, young children begin to show increasing independence and obvious pleasure in moving, communicating and learning through play.

Walkers, Talkers and Pretenders (24-36 months)

From twenty four to thirty six months, children's competence at moving, talking and pretending is more and more evident and they show increasing confidence in themselves and skill in making relationships.

Let's refer back to the table about Roza's progress over a year on page 29.

Using the Birth to Three Framework guidance, how can we see how Roza is developing across the aspects?

A key message within the Framework is that *'children's learning does not fit neatly into separate compartments. As children are strong, competent at learning and playing and skilful communicators at the same time, you will need to consider all aspects to plan effectively for the children in your care'*.

Read the section about Roza's progress over three terms and then look at the aspects and components;

you will see that, as she is under 8 months of age, she is described as a Heads Up, Looker and Communicator (0-8 months). She is reacting to people and situations with her whole body. She is also competent in observing and responding to her immediate environment and communicating with those around her. Refer to the prime areas of development in the revised EYFS:

- Personal, Social and Emotional Development

- Communication and Language

- Physical Development.

What do we understand about Roza's development in the prime areas from the information we have?

Firstly, we need to be clear about what we understand about the prime areas for babies – from birth, these areas develop quickly in response to relationships and experiences.

Personal, Social and Emotion Development is about how babies increasingly develop a positive sense of

themselves, forming positive relationships with those closest to them.

Communication and Language involves babies having opportunities to experience a rich language environment, so that they can start to develop their own confidence and skills in expressing themselves.

Physical Development is about providing babies with opportunities to be active, to develop their co-ordination, control and movement.

Roza is developing a positive relationship with her key worker, she is developing skills in communicating with the adults close to her, and she is offered opportunities to be active.

Roza is showing increasing confidence in trying new experiences; she is supported to lie on the mat and to try and reach for the toys.

When you think of each child as unique, you:

- know about how children develop

- observe children closely

- actively and attentively listen to children and their parents, with respect, whatever their background

- can put yourself in the child's or parents shoes by stepping outside of yourself and seeing things form their point of view – often described as 'empathy'.

Source: *Social and Emotional Aspects of Development,* National Strategies.

What do we already know, through the EYFS (2008), about children's development?

'All children are different and to reflect this, age ranges (in the Development Matters guidance document) have been overlapped in the EYFS to create broad developmental phases. This emphasises that each child's progress is individual to them and that different children develop at different rates. A child does not suddenly move from one phase to another, and they do not make progress in all areas at the same time. However, there are some important 'steps' for each child to take along their own developmental pathway. There are six broad developmental phases'.

0-11 months

During this period, young children's physical development is very rapid and they gain increasing control of their muscles. They also develop skills in moving their hands, feet, limbs and head, quickly becoming mobile and able to handle and manipulate objects. They are learning from the moment of birth. Even before their first words they find out a lot about language by hearing people talking, and are especially interested when it involves themselves and their daily lives. Sensitive care giving, which responds to children's growing understanding and emotional needs, helps to build secure attachments to special people, such as parents, family members or carers. Regular, though flexible, routines help young children to gain a sense of order in the world and to anticipate events. A wide variety of experience, which involves all the senses, encourages learning and an interest in the environment.

8-20 months

As children become mobile new opportunities for exploration and exercise open up. A safe and interesting environment, with age-appropriate resources, helps children to develop curiosity, coordination and physical abilities. This is a time when children can start to learn the beginnings of self-control and how to relate to other people. In this period children can be encouraged to develop their social and mental skills by people to whom they have a positive attachment. Building on their communication skills, children now begin to develop a sense of self and are more able to express their needs and feelings. Alongside non-verbal communication children learn a few simple words for everyday things and people. With encouragement and plenty of interaction with carers, children's communication skills grow and their vocabulary expands very rapidly during this period.

16-26 months

Children in this phase are usually full of energy and need careful support to use it well. Growing physical strengths and skills mean that children need active times for exercise, and quiet times for calmer activities. Playing with other children is an important new area for learning. This helps children to better understand other people's thoughts and feelings, and to learn how to cooperate with others. Exploration and simple self-help builds a sense of self-confidence. Children are also learning about boundaries and how to handle frustration. Play with toys that come apart and fit together encourages problem solving and simple planning. Pretend play helps children to learn about a range of possibilities. Adults are an important source of security and comfort.

22-36 months

Children's fine motor skills continue to develop and they enjoy making marks, using a variety of materials, looking at picture books and listening to stories – important steps in literacy. Self-help and independence soon emerge if adults support and encourage children in areas such as eating, dressing and toileting. Praise for new achievements helps to build their self-esteem. In this phase, children's language is developing rapidly and many are beginning to put sentences together. Joining in conversations with children is an important way for children to learn new things and to begin to think about past, present and future. Developing physical skills mean that children can now usually walk, climb and run, and join in active play with other children. This is an important time for learning about dangers and safe limits.

30-50 months

An increased interest in joint play such as make-believe, construction and games helps children to learn the important social skills of sharing and cooperating. Children also learn more about helping adults in everyday activities and finding a balance between independence and complying with the wishes of others. Children still need the comfort and security of special people. Close, warm relationships with carers form the basis for much learning, such as encouraging children to make healthy choices in food and exercise. At this stage children are becoming more aware of their place in a community. Literacy and numeracy can develop rapidly with the support of a wide range of interesting materials and activities. Children's language is now much more complex, as many become adept at using longer sentences. Conversations with adults become a more important source of information, guidance and reassurance.

40-60 months+

During this period children are now building a stronger sense of their own identity and their place in a wider

world. Children are learning to recognise the importance of social rules and customs, to show understanding and tolerance of others, and to learn how to be more controlled in their own behaviour. Learning and playing in small groups helps to foster the development of social skills. Children now become better able to plan and undertake more challenging activities with a wider range of materials for making and doing. In this phase children learn effectively in shared activities with more able peers and adults. Literacy and problem solving, reasoning and numeracy skills continue to develop.

Children's developing understanding of cause and effect is encouraged by the introduction of a wider variety of equipment, media and technologies.

Inspections from September 2012

In July 2012, Ofsted published the 'Evaluation Schedule' which provides guidance and descriptions for the judgements that inspectors will report on when carrying out inspections for early years providers from

September 2012. Oftsed have also published their 'Conducting Early Years Inspections' document. Both documents can be found on the Ofsted website. The 'Conducting Early Years Inspections' document provides guidance for inspectors conducting inspections under sections 49 and 50 of the Childcare Act 2006 from the time the inspection is arranged to the publication of the report. Inspectors should use this guidance in conjunction with the Evaluation Schedule.

So, what will need to be considered? The Evaluation Schedule covers guidance for inspectors – this guidance is not exhaustive, but it is intended to assist inspectors on the range and type of evidence they might collect. As a guide for settings, it is useful to know what inspectors will refer to, and it may also help you in your preparations for inspections from September 2012.

Inspection judgements

Inspectors will judge the overall quality and standards of the early years provision, taking into account three key judgements:

- how well the early years provision <u>meets the needs</u> of the range of children who attend it

- the contribution of the early years provision to <u>children's well-being</u>

- the <u>leadership and management</u> of the early years provision

Let's look at each of these:

Meeting children's needs

Inspectors will focus on how well individual children benefit from their early years experience. It is important to test your response to individual needs by observing how well you help all children to make effective progress.

Inspectors will evaluate how well you meet the needs of the range of children who attend. They will consider:

- the impact you have on the children's learning and development, whether children make the best possible progress taking into account their starting points and capabilities, the length of time they have been at the setting, and how often they attend.

Inspectors will look for evidence during the inspection to help them reach their overall judgements on your provision. Their grades are: OUTSTANDING (1) GOOD (2) SATISFACTORY (3) INADEQUATE (4).

So, how will the inspector evaluate how well you meet the needs of the children who attend your setting?

The main evidence will come from inspectors' direct observations of the way in which children engage with their environment through play, exploration and active learning, and your input in making learning possible.

Inspectors should supplement their direct observations with a range of other evidence to enable them to evaluate the impact that you have on the progress children make in their learning. This should include:

- evidence of assessment that includes the progress of different groups of children:

  O assessment on entry, including parental contributions

  O two-year-old progress checks (where applicable)

  O ongoing (formative) assessments, including any parental contributions

  O the Early Years Foundation Stage Profile (where applicable) or any other summative assessment when children leave

- evidence of planning for children's next stages of learning based on your assessment and a secure knowledge of the characteristics of learning and children's development

- evidence from observations, including:

  O the inspector's own observations of children's responses to activities

  O any joint observations with managers or early years professionals

  O any evidence of practitioners' observations

- the inspector's tracking of selected children, including children of different ages, funded two-year-olds and other children whose circumstances may suggest they need particular intervention or support

- discussions with practitioners, key persons, managers, parents and children.

It is worth noting that joint observations are being introduced into the inspection process. This will be helpful in encouraging a two-way dialogue between the inspector and the nominated person about what they have jointly seen.

How can you prepare for the inspection? Consider ways in which you could:

- consistently achieve very high standards across all aspects of your work with exceptional educational programmes for children of all ages. Think about how you could inspire others through your own practice

Children's well-being

Inspectors will focus on:

● the effectiveness of your care practices in helping children feel emotionally secure and ensuring children are physically, mentally and emotionally healthy.

So, how will the inspector evaluate the effectiveness of your care practices?

The main evidence comes from inspectors' direct observations of care practices, children's behaviour and their interactions with practitioners and each other. Inspectors should supplement their direct observations with a range of other evidence to enable them to evaluate the impact that you have on children's well-being. This should include:

● evidence of planning for the prime areas of learning and especially for children's personal, social and emotional development

● evidence of assessment of children's well-being

● discussions with practitioners, children and parents and with managers about the key person system

● the inspectors' tracking of children's care arrangements.

In terms of care practices, how can you prepare for the inspection? Consider ways in which you could:

● ensure that you and all practitioners in your setting are highly skilled and sensitive in helping children form secure emotional attachments, and provide a strong base for their developing independence and exploration

● support children to be able to show increasingly high levels of self-control during activities and confidence in social situations, and are developing an excellent understanding of how to manage risks and challenges relative to their age

● consistently give the highest priority to the safety of children and effectively support children's growing

● provide rich, varied and imaginative experiences for children – is this delivered by practitioners in your setting who have very high expectations of themselves and the children, expert knowledge of the areas of learning, and a clear understanding of how children learn?

● focus clearly on assessment at all ages and include all those involved in the child's learning. Do you monitor your observations to use them for timely interventions and support, based on a comprehensive knowledge of the child and their family?

● motivate children to be very eager to join in and consistently demonstrate the characteristics of effective learning. How do you focus on helping children to acquire communication and language skills, and on supporting their physical, personal, social and emotional development? Your aim should be to prepare children exceptionally well for school or the next steps in their learning

● engage all parents in their children's learning in your setting and at home using highly successful strategies.

understanding of how to keep themselves safe and healthy

- provide a highly stimulating environment with child-accessible resources that promote learning and challenge children both in and outdoors

- demonstrate strong skills to show that all children are well prepared for the next stages in their learning. Do you skilfully support children's transitions both within the setting and/or to other settings and school?

The effectiveness of leadership and management

Inspectors will focus on:

- the effectiveness of the leadership and management in understanding and implementing the requirements of the Early Years Foundation Stage.

So, how will the inspector evaluate the effectiveness of your leadership and management?

The main evidence comes from interviews with the manager and/or registered provider or their nominee, supplemented by discussion with staff and parents and, if needed, sampling of policies and procedures. Inspectors should obtain evidence of:

- how well practitioners and any trainees or students are monitored, coached, mentored and supported, and how under-performance is tackled

- the effectiveness of a programme of professional development arising from identified staff needs

- the extent and range of completed training, including child protection and the impact of that training in improving children's well-being

- the effectiveness of the staff's monitoring and revision of the educational programmes to ensure that they have sufficient depth, breadth and challenge, and reflect the needs, aptitudes and interest of children

- the effectiveness of the monitoring of children's progress and interventions, where needed, to ensure that gaps are narrowing for groups of children or individual children identified as being in need of support

- the effectiveness of arrangements for safeguarding, including recruitment practices and how well safe practices and a culture of safety are promoted and understood

- how well required policies and procedures are implemented

- the effectiveness of self-evaluation, including contributions from parents, carers and other stakeholders

- whether well-focused improvement plans have been implemented through engagement with staff, children, parents and carers

- the effectiveness of arrangements for information sharing and partnership working with other providers, schools and professionals in order to

identify all children's needs and help them to make progress.

- Inspectors must use their professional judgement to interpret and apply the grade descriptions for childminders.

In terms of leadership and management, how can you prepare for the inspection? Consider ways in which you could:

- demonstrate how you inspire others through your leadership. Do you focus on achieving excellence throughout your setting – how do you show through well documented records that you continuously aim to improve on your achievements, or maintain the highest levels of achievement, for all children, over a sustained period of time?

- describe your excellent understanding of your responsibility to ensure that your setting meets the safeguarding and welfare requirements of the Early Years Foundation Stage, and that you have effective systems to monitor their implementation

- provide high quality professional supervision, based on consistent and sharply focused evaluations of the impact of your staff's practice. Do you have a targeted programme of professional development to ensure that your staff are constantly improving their understanding and practice?

- identify children's needs quickly. Do you ensure that you have highly effective partnerships between the setting, parents, external agencies and other providers?

Inspectors will consider the overall quality and standards of your setting – they will take account of all the judgements made across the evaluation schedule. In particular, inspectors must consider:

- the progress all children make in their learning and development relative to their starting points and their readiness for the next stage of their education

- the extent to which the learning and care provided by the setting meets the needs of the range of children who attend, including the needs of any children who have special educational needs and/or disabilities

- children's personal and emotional development, including whether they feel safe and are secure and happy

- whether the requirements for children's safeguarding and welfare have been met

- the effectiveness of leadership and management in evaluating practice and securing continuous improvement that improves children's life chances.

Think about how you consistently reflect the highest aspirations for all children and staff, enable children to make excellent progress in relation to their starting points and prepare them well for school or the next stage in their learning.

The 'Conducting Early Years Inspections' document gives further detail about the ways in which inspectors will gather and record evidence:

> *'The inspector must spend as much time as possible observing a wide range of activities and care routines, talking to practitioners and children about what they are doing and evaluating children's understanding and engagement in their learning. In setting up the inspection the*

inspector should engage the provider in the inspection and explain how and where evidence will be gathered'.

In the past, some settings had reported that some inspectors had spent very little time actually observing staff with children and had focused their attention more on the paperwork. From September 2012, there will be far more emphasis on the inspector observing care practices, how children are being supported in their learning and how their needs are being met. This is a welcome development for many settings who are proud of what they offer – so what will the inspector do differently? The main difference will be the joint observations:

Joint observations help:

- the inspector to gain an insight into the effectiveness of the provision's professional development programme for practitioners

- the inspector to assess the accuracy and quality of the provider's staff's monitoring and evaluation of practice

- the provider to contribute evidence towards judgements about the quality of practice and learning.

How will these joint observations be arranged? If joint observations are undertaken, the inspector and the provider should agree which activities/age groups/ care routines to select. After the observation they should discuss their views about the quality of practice in supporting children's care, learning and development. The inspector should not convey a view about the activity and/or care routine initially, but should ask the provider for their view about its strengths, what would have made it better and how good it was overall.

Where the quality of practice is weak, it is important that the inspector talks to the provider about what has been observed. The inspector should also ask about the action the provider is taking, if any, to bring about improvement. After joint observations, the inspector and the provider should agree how to manage feedback to the practitioner and when this should take place. The inspector may ask the provider to give feedback to the practitioner(s) in order to evaluate the manager's assessment about the quality of practice observed.

If providers offer a written record of the observation, the inspector should look at this. Any differences in the analysis of practice should be explored. Following a joint observation, the inspector should record evidence in the usual way. Any comments about the quality of the provider's evaluation should be included on the inspector's evidence. Any notes taken by the provider should not be taken away or included within the evidence base.

Where childminders work alone it is not possible to carry out joint observations. The inspector may wish to engage in observation of a specific activity planned by the childminder, and discuss with the childminder the aims of the activity and the learning intentions. The inspector should follow this up with a further discussion about what the child has learnt and the next steps. Where childminders have assistants, a joint observation of one assistant may be possible.

Tracking

In group provision the inspector must track a representative sample of children. As a minimum, the

a child who speaks English as an additional language

a boy and/or girl from any groups who may be disadvantaged, for example the children of travellers or asylum seekers.

Evidence from case tracking must include:

observation notes, assessment and planning for each child including the progress check for any children aged two

discussions with each child's key person and information about progress over time

any records kept by the provision that show how they have tracked the progress children make, including any concerns about the children's development in the prime and/or specific areas of learning

an evaluation of the accuracy and rigour of the provision's assessments and the extent to which children's next steps in learning are well planned.

Inspectors should also observe the tracked children in order to evaluate:

the range of activities children take part in, whether solitary, self-initiated or adult-initiated

the quality and timeliness of adults' interventions

the level of challenge of the activities for the children's age/stage of development

the development levels at which they are working, including whether they are exceeding, reaching, or are likely to reach, expected levels of development (as shown in Development Matters)

ways in which communication and language are developed and literacy taught

whether children are developing skills in the prime areas that help them to be ready for school

how well any learning they demonstrate is built upon by the adults working with them

inspector must track two children. This number will increase where a provision has a wide age range of children, where children are in different rooms and/or where there are distinct groups of children. The inspector should identify children who have attended the provision for a reasonable period of time as this should mean that the provider has established the children's starting points and evaluated the progress they are making.

The inspector may include in the sample:

a baby

a funded two-year-old child

a boy and girl who are soon to transfer to school

children the provision identifies as having differing abilities

a looked after child, if applicable

a child with disabilities and/or special educational needs

- their care arrangements, including intimate care, the levels of privacy afforded to the child, supervision arrangements for the child and for the adult undertaking personal hygiene tasks

- longer observations over 30 minutes, for example in the baby room. The inspector may wish to conduct longer observations in order to assess care routines and activities and how well these are supporting children's secure attachments. The inspector may wish to carry out longer observations in order to capture the best practice, or to diagnose weaker areas of practice and provide detailed evidence to underpin recommendations for improvement

- short observations of a number of activities. This approach is helpful where all the children are situated in one room and move around activities depending on their interests.

Making judgements

The evaluation schedule sets out the judgements that the inspector must make and the aspects they should consider when doing so. The inspector must use professional judgement to weigh up the available evidence and reach judgements that fairly and reliably reflect the quality of the early years provision. The inspector is not expected to check that each requirement of the Early Years Foundation Stage is being met. However, if in the course of collecting evidence the inspector finds that a particular requirement is not being met they should take this into account when reaching judgements.

Legislation other than the Early Years Foundation Stage

In addition to meeting the Early Years Foundation Stage requirements (refer to the Statutory Framework) providers must also comply with other relevant legislation. This includes safeguarding legislation, and legislation relating to employment, anti-discrimination, health and safety and data collection. Where the inspector identifies concerns that may also relate to other legislation s/he must notify the compliance, investigation and enforcement team, who will decide what action should be taken, and whether there should

be liaison with the appropriate agencies. Your local authority adviser will be able to guide you on matters relating to current legislation, and may also offer training on some of the areas highlighted above. The ACAS website (www.acas.org.uk) is useful for employment issues and your Local Children's Safeguarding Board will provide you with guidance to support you in keeping children safe.

Policies and procedures

The inspector does not need to check all the policies, procedures and documentation but should check a small sample including:

- the record of Criminal Records Bureau (CRB) checks and a selection of recruitment records (where applicable)

- qualifications, including paediatric First Aid (to ensure ratio and qualification requirements are met and whether these in turn are having an impact on the quality of provision)

Inspectors should be familiar with these materials. While there may not be a direct correlation between the judgements of the local authority and those of inspectors, inspection evidence must take into account the views of other professionals on the quality of the provision for young children'.

This means that your local authority advisers are expected to offer support to all settings using an open process – you need to know whether or not you are receiving extra support to help you improve.

Described here as either universal, targeted or intensive support, your local authority may instead use what is known as a RAG rating – i.e. red, amber or green, to determine which level of support you may need.

Source: *(Ofsted) Early Years Schedule, Conducting Early Years Inspections.*

- a sample of induction, training and professional development records

- a sample of planning and assessment documents

- the complaints record

- the provision's self-evaluation where not already submitted to Ofsted, including the local authority development officer's most recent report on the provision and any quality rating or categorisation.

So, what is the role of the local authority?

'Local authorities are expected to categorise provision through a transparent open process and use the information from this to offer universal, targeted and intensive support to help providers improve. Local authorities may continue to use the Early Years Quality Improvement Programme document or the Early Childhood Environment Rating Scales.

Section Three:
Leadership and support

Quality in the Setting

Leadership affects the whole provision. How do you raise the quality and maintain the service you provide? How can you ensure effective implementation of the revised EYFS Framework? The following are points for managers/ senior staff to consider. Remember, 'quality' is all about every aspect of your work.

1. **How effective is your setting in securing a high quality environment for learning?**

   Consider how you all meet the needs of each unique child and support all areas of their learning and development.

2. **How effective are your staff in supporting each child's progress and learning?**

Consider how you guide staff in organising their planning for individual children, how you can evaluate the quality of the adult support for children's learning experiences and how they may effectively assess children's progress.

3. **How effective is your leadership?**

   Consider your own knowledge and understanding of the legal framework, how you plan for improvement and how you lead others in the setting to improve the provision.

4. **How effective are you in developing practitioner learning?**

   Consider each member of staff individually – their confidence and abilities, and what training and continuing professional development may be most appropriate for them.

Early Years is now a graduate-led profession. There has been emphasis in recent years to develop the workforce in terms of their qualifications – although experience should be recognised and valued too.

The sector has worked hard to ensure that the role of the early years practitioner is recognised as being more than 'just' looking after children! When you support your staff to gain qualifications, and support them in their CPD (Continuous Professional Development) you are ensuring that your setting can provide quality care and early learning experiences for all children.

So, what are 'qualifications', and what is 'continuous professional development' (CPD)?

Simply, qualifications are awards that are made once a practitioner has successfully studied over a period of time. CPD keeps the practitioner's knowledge current, such as refresher courses on first aid, which needs to be updated every three years.

5. How effective is your setting in facilitating partnerships for learning?

Consider how you can develop and maintain a learning 'culture' and how you can work with and involve others beyond the setting.

Ultimately, think about the impact your leadership has on outcomes for children – after all, it is all about the care and development of the children for whom you are responsible.

Professional Development

'The daily experience of children in early years settings and the overall quality of provision depends on practitioners having appropriate qualifications, training, skills and knowledge and a clear understanding of their roles and responsibilities'.

Refer to the revised Statutory Framework for the EYFS, pages 16-17.

'In group settings, the manager must hold at least a full and relevant level 3 qualification and at least half of all other staff must hold at least a full and relevant level 2 qualification. The manager should have at least two years' experience of working in an early years setting, or have at least two years' other suitable experience. The provider must ensure there is a named deputy who, in their judgement, is capable and qualified to take charge in the manager's absence'.

'Providers should ensure that regular staff appraisals are carried out to identify any training needs, and secure opportunities for continuous professional development for staff. Providers should support their staff to improve their qualification levels wherever possible'.

You will see references to what are described as 'full and relevant' qualifications. This can be confusing – you can refer to the Teaching Agency website (www.education.gov.uk) that defines what is meant by 'full and relevant' when you are considering which qualification is most suitable for the individual member of staff.

On pages 48 and 49, you will see **EXAMPLES only** of qualifications from Level 1 through to Level 6 for Early Years and Playwork (where applicable).

Remember – the role of the practitioner is to care for children and to support their learning. Practitioners (at all levels) need to continue and progress with their own learning too! This is sometimes described as 'lifelong learning'

Foundations for Quality

The independent review of early education and childcare qualifications (Final Report) was published in June 2012, Cathy Nutbrown led the review. She says:

'Our present qualifications system does not always equip practitioners with the knowledge and experience necessary for them to offer children high quality care and education, and to support professional development throughout their careers. Changes are needed, and I have made 19 recommendations for how I believe this should be done – some for Government to consider, and others I hope the sector will take forward. The quality of children's experiences are at the core of this report and an important part of this is the status of the early years workforce in society. Early years carers and educators are professionals who need to be able continually to develop their knowledge, skills and understanding. They need to be confident in their own practice and in engaging with other professionals, such as health visitors and social workers'.

The review is of current interest to all practitioners working in the early years sector.

Early Years

The table on page 48 shows EXAMPLES of qualifications – refer to the Teaching Agency website for more information. (On 1 April 2012, the Teaching Agency became a new executive agency of the Department for Education. Some of the work previously undertaken by the CWDC (Children's Workforce Development Council) is now being done through the Teaching Agency).

Please be aware that although CACHE has been used within the examples in the table, there are other awarding bodies that offer these courses too. Your local training provider will be able to help you with this.

Most of the Early Years courses shown here are on the QCF (Qualifications and Credit Framework). The QCF is a system for recognising skills and qualifications. It does this by awarding credit for qualifications and units (small steps of learning). Each unit has a credit value. This value specifies the number of credits gained by learners who complete that unit. The flexibility of the system allows learners to gain qualifications at their own pace along routes that suit them best. Each learner has a Unique Learner Number (ULN) by which they are identified.

(EYPS: Early Years Professional Status; QTS: Qualified Teacher Status.)

Playwork

Again, these are EXAMPLES only, refer to the Teaching Agency website for more information. As with the Early Years courses, you need to be aware that although CACHE has been used in the examples, there are other awarding bodies that offer these courses too. Your local training provider will be able to help you with this.

Qualifications table: Early Years

LEVELS

Early Years	1	2	3	4	5	6	EYPS and QTS
Course	Cache Level 1 Award, Certificate and Diploma in Introduction to Health, Social Care and Children's and Young People's Settings (QCF) — non work based, part-time	Cache Level 2 Certificate and Diploma for the Children and Young People workforce (QCF) — work based and/or full time	Cache Level 3 Diploma for the Children and Young People's workforce (QCF) — work based and /or full time	Certificate in Early Years Practice (Open University) — distance learning	Foundation Degree in Children's Development and Learning (University of Reading) — work based	BA Children's Development and Learning (University of Reading) — work based	EYPS – is the only graduate accreditation for the early years workforce which is recognised as the credential for leading practice in early years provision (CWDC) / QTS – is the accreditation that enables you to teach in state maintained and special schools in England and Wales (Teaching Agency)
Suitable for	Anyone considering a career in health and/or social care with adults or children and young people	Anyone who wants to work, or has just started to work in the children and young people's workforce	Anyone who works or wants to work at a supervisory level in the children and young people's workforce	Anyone who works with children aged birth-7 years and wants to develop their practice	Foundation Degrees provide a model of vocational higher education based on close collaboration between employers and providers of Higher Education. It is a work based programme studied over 2 years. The Foundation Degree is validated as a Level 5 award and is suitable for Level 3 practitioners working in an early years/ educational setting who wish to progress their chosen career	Students holding a Foundation Degree. The BA CDL provides a model of vocational Higher Education based on a close matching of academic study to relevant employment based tasks. Modules are generic and can be accessed by practitioners working with children from the EYFS (Birth- 5) to Key Stage 3 (11-14). The programme enables Foundation Degree students to progress to Honours within one year	EYPS – for graduate practitioners who have responsibility for leading practice and curriculum delivery within early years provision. Practitioners can also gain EYPS alongside the final year of a three year degree programme / QTS – practitioners need to complete a period of Initial Teacher Training which supports the professional standards for QTS
Job roles on completion	This qualification does not allow a person to work unsupervised with children, but it does provide a starting point for deciding whether a career in the sector is the way forward	Assistant pre-school worker. Assistant in children's centres. Assistant in a children's residential care home. Assistant in day nurseries, nursery schools, or reception classes in primary schools	Pre-school worker. Practitioner in a Children's Centre. Practitioner in day nurseries, nursery schools and primary schools	Practitioner working with greater responsibilities with children aged between birth-7 years	Practitioners with leadership responsibility within early years provision, including full day care, pre-school, out of school settings, nurseries and home based childcare such as childminders. Practitioners can progress onto a BA Hons Degree	Practitioners with leadership responsibility within early years and support roles within Key Stage 1 to 3. Practitioners can progress onto EYPS and/or PGCE	EYPS – Lead practitioners for the EYFS within a variety of early years provision including full day care, pre-school, nurseries, children centres, out of school settings and home based childcare such as childminders. Advisors roles within national and local organisations / QTS – Qualified teacher within state maintained and special schools (England and Wales), children centres and early years provision

Qualifications table: **Playwork**

LEVELS

Playwork	1	2	3	4	5	6 and 7
Course	Take 5 for Play Part time 15 hours	Cache Level 2 Award and Certificate in Playwork.(QCF) Cache Level 2 diploma in Playwork.(QCF) Part time	Cache Level 3 Award in induction to playwork (QCF) Cache Level 3 Certificate in playwork (QCF) Cache Level 3 Diploma in Playwork (QCF) Cache Level 3 Award in Transition from Early Years to Playwork Part time	Level 4 Award and Certificate in Playwork (QCF) Part time	Level 5 Diploma in Playwork (QCF) (University of Gloucester) Part time	BA and MA Playwork (QCF) www.playworkpartnerships.co.uk The University of Gloucestershire offers a variety of accessible Higher Education qualifications for people working in the playwork field. All are offered part time, via distance learning. Qualifications include: Certificate of Higher Education in Playwork Diploma of Higher Education in Playwork; BA Hons Degree in Playwork; Graduate Diploma in Playwork; Postgraduate Certificate in Play and Playwork MA in Play and Playwork Part time
Suitable for	Anyone who wants to work with children in or out of school settings	Anyone who wishes to work in a supervised role in a wide range of playwork environments	Experienced playworkers who have a wide knowledge and understanding of children and young people and an appreciation of playwork principles and practice	Playworkers who have a wide knowledge and understanding of children and young people and a deep appreciation of playwork principles and practice	Playworkers who have a wide knowledge and understanding of children and young people and a deep appreciation of playwork principles and practice	Those who want to take playwork to a higher level
Job roles on completion	Assistant in play setting	Assistant in play setting	Those managing playwork settings	Leading and managing others in playwork settings	Leading and managing others in playwork settings	Professional practitioners

Most of the Playwork courses shown here are on the QCF. The QCF is a system for recognising skills and qualifications. It does this by awarding credit for qualifications and units (small steps of learning). Each unit has a credit value. This value specifies the number of credits gained by learners who complete that unit. The flexibility of the system allows learners to gain qualifications at their own pace along routes that suit them best. Each learner has a Unique Learner Number (ULN) by which they are identified.

Effective practice

Effective practice is something all practitioners should aspire to. The KEEP statements are a reminder of what effective practice is all about:

KEEP
(Key Elements of Effective Practice)

Effective practice in the early years requires committed, enthusiastic and reflective practitioners with a breadth and depth of knowledge, skills and understanding.

Effective practitioners use their own learning to improve their work with young children and their families in ways which are sensitive, positive and non-judgemental.

Therefore, through initial and on-going training and development, practitioners need to develop, demonstrate and continuously improve their:

- relationships with both children and adults

- understanding of the individual and diverse ways that children develop and learn

- knowledge and understanding in order to actively support and extend children's learning in and across all areas and aspects of learning

- practice in meeting all children's needs, learning styles and interests

- work with parents, carers and the wider community

- work with other professionals within and beyond the setting.

The early years and childcare workforce need appropriate skills and knowledge to be effective practitioners:

The Common Core of Skills and Knowledge promote equality, respect diversity and challenge stereotypes, helping to improve life chances for all children, including those who have disabilities and those who are most vulnerable:

- effective communication and engagement

- child and young person development

- safeguarding and promoting the welfare of the child

- supporting transitions

- multi-agency working

- sharing information.

Let's consider two of the areas of the Common Core skills and knowledge.

Child and young person development

The Common Core of Skills and Knowledge for the Children's Workforce state that the core area covers the physical, intellectual, linguistic, social and emotional growth and development of babies, children and young people. It is difficult to determine specific times when developmental changes occur, as these will differ from person to person.

What is important is a basic understanding of those changes and how they can affect a baby, child or young person's behaviour. Parents and carers may be well placed to identify developmental and behavioural changes in their children but they may also find them difficult to cope with and seek reassurance, information, advice and support at various stages. It is therefore important that you have the ability to self-reflect and adjust your own behaviour appropriately.

Skills

Observation and judgement

- Observe a child or young person's behaviour, understand its context, and notice any unexpected changes.

- Listen actively and respond to concerns expressed about developmental or behavioural changes.

- Record observations in an appropriate manner.

- Understand that babies, children and young people see and experience the world in different ways.

- Evaluate the situation, taking into consideration the individual, their situation and development issues.

- Be able to recognise the signs of a possible developmental delay.

- Be able to support children and young people with a developmental difficulty or disability, and understand that their families, parents and carers will also need support and reassurance. Approach this with sensitivity and respect, and with recognition that children and their families have feelings.

- Make considered decisions on whether concerns can be addressed by providing or signposting additional sources of information or advice.

- Where you feel that further support is needed, know when to take action yourself and when to refer to managers, supervisors or other relevant professionals

- Be able to distinguish between fact and opinion.

Empathy and understanding

- Demonstrate your commitment to reaching a shared understanding with a child, young person, parent or carer by talking and listening effectively; make sensitive judgements about what is being said and what is meant by what is being said.

- Be able to support a child or young person to reach their own decisions (while taking into account health and safety and child protection issues).

Understand how babies, children and young people develop

- Know that development includes emotional, physical, intellectual, social, moral and character growth, and know that they can all affect one another.

- Appreciate the different ways in which babies and children form attachments and how these might change.

- Recognise that play and recreation directed by babies, children and young people, not adults play a major role in helping them understand themselves and the world around them as well as helping them realise their potential.

- Know how to interact with children in ways that support the development of their ability to think and learn.

Be clear about your own job role

- Know who the experts are and when they are needed.

- Remember that parents and carers almost always know their children best.

- Know how to obtain support and report concerns.

- Have a broad knowledge of the laws and key policy areas related to children.

- Know about the Child Health Promotion Programme and Common Assessment Framework for Children and Young People (CAF) and, where appropriate, how to use them. Information about the Child Health Promotion Programme can be found on the Department of Health (DH) website (www.dh.gov.uk). *'The CAF is a key part of delivering frontline services that are integrated and focused around the needs of children'*. Department for Education

Know how to reflect and improve

- Know how to use theory and experience to reflect upon, think about and improve your practice.

- Highlight additional training and supervision needs to build on your skills and knowledge.

- Encourage a child or young person to value their personal experiences and knowledge.

- Appreciate the impact of transitions on child development.

Knowledge

Understand context

- Know and recognise the child or young person's position in a family or caring network, as well as a wider social context, and appreciate the diversity of these networks.

- Understand and take account of the effects of different parenting approaches, backgrounds and routines.

- Know and recognise that for some children and young people, delayed or disordered development may stem from underlying, potentially undiagnosed disability and is not a reflection of parenting skills.

- Understand and behave appropriately for the baby, child or young person's stage of development.

- Be aware that working with children and young people may affect you emotionally and know some sources of help in dealing with the impact of this.

- Draw upon your experience and others' perspectives to enable you to challenge your thinking and assess the impact of your actions.

- Know your role in supporting and promoting development.

- Know how to motivate and encourage children and young people to achieve their full potential and how to empower and encourage parents and carers to do the same.

Safeguarding and promoting the welfare of the child

The Common Core of Skills and Knowledge for the Children's Workforce states that those who work with children and young people have a responsibility to safeguard and promote their welfare. This is an important responsibility and requires vigilance. You will need to be able to recognise when a child or young person may not be achieving their developmental potential or their health may be impaired, and be able to identify appropriate sources of help for them and their families.

It is important to identify concerns as early as possible so that children, young people, their families and carers can get the help they need. As well as ensuring that children and young people are free from harm, it is equally important to ensure their well-being and quality of life is maintained.

Skills

Relate, recognise and take considered action

- Establish a rapport and respectful, trusting relationships with children, young people and those caring for them.

- Understand what is meant by safeguarding and the different ways in which children and young people can be harmed (including by other children and

young people), apply careful supervision when using the Internet.

- Make considered judgements about how to act to safeguard and promote a child or young person's welfare, where appropriate consulting with the child, young person, parent or carer to inform your thinking.

- Give the child or young person the opportunity to participate in decisions affecting them, as appropriate to their age and ability, and taking their wishes and feelings into account.

- Understand the key role of parents and carers in safeguarding and promoting children and young people's welfare and involve them accordingly, while recognising factors that can affect parenting and increase the risk of abuse (for example, domestic violence).

- Understand that signs of abuse can be subtle and be expressed in play, artwork and in the way children and young people approach relationships with other children and/or adults.

- Make considered judgements about how to act to safeguard and promote a child or young person's welfare.

- Give the child or young person the opportunity to participate in decisions affecting them, as appropriate to their age and ability.

Communication, recording and reporting

- Use the appropriate IT and language skills to effectively observe, record and report, making a distinction between observation, facts, information gained from others and opinion.

- Undertake (formal or informal) assessments and be alert to concerns about a child or young person's safety or welfare, including unexplained changes in behaviour and signs of abuse or neglect. Understanding the issues from the child's perspective is crucial.

- Be able to recognise when a child or young person is in danger or at risk of harm, and take action to protect them.

Personal skills

- Have self-awareness and the ability to analyse objectively. Have the confidence to represent actively the child or young person and his or her rights.

- Have the confidence to challenge your own and others' practice.

- Understand the different forms and extent of abuse and their impact on children's development.

- Develop appropriate professional relationships with children and young people.

Knowledge

Legal and procedural frameworks

- Have awareness and basic knowledge, where appropriate, of the most current legislation.

- Know about Government and local guidance, policies and procedure and how they apply these in the wider working environment.

- Be aware of the Local Safeguarding Children Board and its remit.

- Be aware of national guidance and local procedures, and your own role and responsibilities within these for safeguarding and promoting children and young people's welfare.

- Know about data protection issues in the context of your role.

Wider context of services

- Know when and how to discuss concerns with parents and carers. This can be sensitive for all involved, and support may be needed for practitioners. Think about circumstances when you might not approach parents about concerns – it may be that to do so could place the child at greater risk of harm.

You can always seek guidance/advice from your local LSCB.

- Understand the roles of other agencies, local procedures on child protection and variations in use of terminology.

- Understand the necessity of information sharing within the context of children and young people's well-being and safety.

- Know about the Common Assessment Framework for Children and Young People (CAF) and, where appropriate, how to use it.

- Understand that different confidentiality procedures may apply in different contexts.

Self-knowledge

- Know the boundaries of personal competence and responsibility, know when to involve others, and know where to get advice and support. At all times, remain professional in your approach and mindful of confidentiality.

- Appreciate the effect of witnessing upsetting situations and know how to get support.

- Know about local resources and how to access information including, where appropriate, a common assessment.

- Understand your own role and its limits, and the importance of providing care or support.

In the slimmed down revised version of the EYFS, the KEEP statements and the Common Core of Skills and Knowledge are not shown. In fact, the Common Core of Skills and Knowledge have been archived, which may give the impression that they are no longer relevant. As with the Every Child Matters agenda, KEEP and the Common Core of Skills and Knowledge do still apply, they are widely used to inform on practice.

The revised EYFS comprises of the Statutory Framework. Alongside the additional guidance, Development Matters and the Know How Guide, other existing guidance will still remain relevant and helpful to you in your work with children in the Early Years Foundation Stage.

In conclusion

The revised EYFS has come about as a result of the recommendations of Dame Claire Tickell. Her comments are a reminder to us all about what our role as practitioners is all about – the children!

'The earliest years in a child's life are absolutely critical. There is overwhelming international evidence that foundations are laid in the first years of life which, if weak, can have a permanent and detrimental impact on children's longer term development. A child's future choices, attainment, wellbeing, happiness and resilience are profoundly affected by the quality of the guidance, love and care they receive during these first years. While children spend considerable amounts of time with their parents or carers during these early years, they also spend increasing amounts of time in a wide range of early years settings. Parents and carers are the people who have the most important influence on children's early development – but evidence shows that good quality early years provision also has a large impact on children's longer term outcomes'.

Acknowledgements

The author would like to thank:

Jo Elsey, Head of Early Years, Institute of Education, University of Reading.

Marian Heelas, Director, Training for You, Hampshire.

Julia Reveler, Lecturer, Early Years and Childcare, Newbury College, Berkshire.

Victoria Park Nursery School and Children's Centre, Newbury, Berkshire.

Little Rainbows Day Nursery, Hungerford, Berkshire.

The author and Practical Pre-School Books would like to thank the Pre-School Learning Alliance for permission to use an edited extract from the Pre-School Learning Alliance publication *Small Messy Play Hands* (2012).

Notes

Notes